Language Readers

Level 3
Book H
Units 43–48

**Jane Fell Greene
Judy Fell Woods**

Copyright 2000 (Third Edition) by Jane Fell Greene and Judy Fell Woods.
All rights reserved.

05 04 03 02   7 6 5 4

ISBN 1-57035-442-1
ISBN 1-57035-277-1 Set

No portion of this work may be reproduced or transmitted in any form or by any means, electronic or mechanical, including photocopying or recording, or by any information storage and retrieval system, without the express written permission of the publisher.

Text layout and design by Kimberly Harris
Cover design by Becky Malone
Cover Image © *2000 by* Artville, LLC
Illustrated by Peggy Ranson

This product is in compliance with AB2519 California State Adoption revision requirements.

Printed in the United States of America

Published and Distributed by

SOPRIS
WEST

4093 Specialty Place • Longmont, CO 80504 • (303) 651-2829
www.sopriswest.com

Contents

Unit 43 The Gold Robbery 1

Unit 44 An Oversight 17

Unit 45 Nothing Ventured, Nothing Gained 33

Unit 46 The Weight of the World 49

Unit 47 The Modern Memphis 71

Unit 48 Knowing Right From Wrong 93

Unit 43

THE GOLD ROBBERY

UNIT 43

Phonology/Orthography Concepts

- Phonograms are letter groups that usually represent the same sounds (phonemes).
- In the phonograms **old** and **oll**, **o** represents the long /o/ phoneme.

Vocabulary

bold	gold	roll	stroll	*flood*
cold	hold	scold	told	*floor*
colder	mold	scroll	troll	
droll	old	smolder		
fold	poll	sold		

THE GOLD ROBBERY

Story Summary:

Hi North has been assigned to give Mr. Grunch, an elderly gentleman, a certificate of appreciation for donating funds to help rebuild Lake School after it had burned down. But when Hi and his brother get to the Grunch house, they find big problems.

It was Saturday, and Hi North remembered his promise to the students and principal of Lake School. He would take the certificate of appreciation to Mr. Grunch this morning.

Mr. Grunch had given a large amount of money to rebuild Lake School after it had burned down. The new school had been built and its principal, staff, and students wanted to give Mr. Grunch a document to honor his generosity. Mr. Grunch was unable to pick up the certificate at the awards ceremony, so Mr. Ade had assigned Hi to deliver it to him.

"It's almost 11:00," Mrs. North reminded Hi. "You should go to Mr. Grunch's before noon."

"Aw, Mom," Hi complained, "do I have to?"

"Come on, Sport," Hi's older brother, Sid, said. "I'll go with you. Sam's coming over to play some basketball, so we'll walk with you."

"Gee, thanks, Sid," Hi sighed. "I was kind of scared. That Grunch house gives me the creeps!"

"I know, Hi," Sid concurred. "It's so scary, especially when the windows are dark. And the way that big old elm tree creeps over the porch."

"Yeah," agreed Hi, "Bud tripped over Mr. Grunch's garbage can because he thought he saw a spooky face in the window. It's creepy!"

"Now boys," Mrs. North cut in, "Mr. Grunch had every right to ask Nick and Bud to stay off his property. I understand just how hard he works on his lawn and garden. He doesn't want anyone trampling over it."

"Well," Sid muttered under his breath, "he doesn't have to act like such a mean old troll."

"That will be enough of that," announced Mrs. North. "Mr. Grunch has saved Lake School and he deserves the certificate. Go! Meet Sam and get on over there! Mr. Ade called him yesterday and said that you would be there before noon."

A shadow darkened the window of the back door. Startled, Hi jumped.

Sam Webster opened the door. "Looks like a great day to get in some basketball practice. You ready, Sid?"

Sid picked up his ball. "OK," he said, "but first we have to go with Hi over to the Grunches' house. Did you walk or ride your bike?"

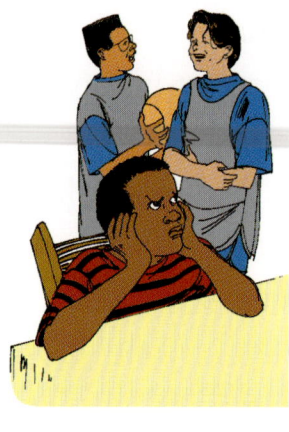

"I rode," Sam replied. "Why does Hi have to go over there?"

"Remember when the old man gave all that money to rebuild Lake School? Well, they made a certificate for him and Hi has to take it over there." Sid grinned gleefully.

"My man Hi!" Sam teased, "Aren't you scared? Everybody's scared to go over there."

As they coasted down Poll Street Hill, the glare of the morning sun blinded them. When they turned the corner into the shadow, they noticed a "Sold" sign on the lawn of their friend Mat's old house. "I miss Mat," Sam said. "Remember how much fun we used to have over there before the Millers moved down by the dock?"

"Yeah," Sid agreed. "But they needed a bigger house. Their baby was pushing them out into the street with all her baby junk!" The boys were still laughing when they arrived at the Grunches'.

"That's funny," Sid noticed, "Mr. Grunch's door is ajar. He never leaves his door open."

"That doesn't sound like Mr. Grunch," added Sam. "But there's only one way to find out."

As they approached the Grunches' wraparound porch, Sid noticed muddy footprints on the doormat. The chairs in the hallway were turned askew and a crystal bud vase lay shattered on a gleaming wooden floor.

"Something's wrong here," Sid cautioned. He hesitated before he knocked and called out, "Mr. and Mrs. Grunch! You here? Anybody home?"

They heard a banging sound coming from inside and tiptoed in to take a look.

Mr. and Mrs. Grunch lay gagged on the floor, hands bound together from behind, the hot sun beating on them through the east window of their living room. "Call 911, Hi," ordered Sam, as he and Sid went to work untying the old couple.

"Mr. Grunch, who did this to you?" asked the boys in unison.

Mr. Grunch stumbled toward his desk.

Mrs. Grunch wavered as Sam untied her.

"Well I never!" Mrs. Grunch breathed hoarsely. "That man knocked me down before I had a chance to see him."

Mr. Grunch was concerned about his wife. "Are you all right, my dear?" he asked.

"Good as I can be after all that!" she replied.

Hi announced that the police were on their way as Mr. Grunch started thumbing through his desk.

"That thief took all my stocks and bonds," he moaned, shaking his head. "My gold coin collection is missing and Mrs. Grunch's jewelry."

"Not the gold coin my grandmother gave me?" sobbed Mrs. Grunch.

"It's all gone, my dear," Mr. Grunch cried out. "A lifetime of savings down the drain. Gone!"

"I've told you a hundred times to take that stuff to the bank," Mrs. Grunch put in, dejectedly.

Sid went to the door to let in Detectives Rozas and Goldman from the Jasper Police Department. Sid took them to the Grunches' living room.

"Do you two need an ambulance?" the detectives inquired as they introduced themselves. Sid and Sam stood back as the detectives took over.

"I'm fine," grunted Mr. Grunch.

"I'm OK," replied Mrs. Grunch. "I'm just mad that I didn't get a look at the thief!" Composed now, Mrs. Grunch was as feisty as ever.

While Goldman combed the area for possible clues, Rozas began questioning the Grunches.

"How about you, Mr. Grunch," inquired Detective Rozas, "did you get a look at the intruder? And are you sure there was only one?"

"There was just one culprit," Mr. Grunch stated. "I only saw him briefly, but he looked to be about 19 or 20. He had black hair with one of those ponytails in back and was wearing a black leather jacket. He knocked me down before I could get a real good look, but I *know* I saw a distinct scar on his face. On his chin. Looked like a corkscrew."

Sid and Sam were listening to the questioning. "Wow, Sam," whispered Sid, "Kim's cousin Kenneth is 19 and he has a scar like that. He's visiting Kim this week, from East Oldham. Should we tell?"

"I don't know, Sid," Sam said. "Kim's a good friend. We wouldn't want to get her into trouble."

"Kim wouldn't be in any trouble. And Mr. and Mrs. Grunch deserve to know who did this to them," Sid contended. "Not to mention getting back the stuff that was stolen from them."

"I still don't think it's right," Sam reiterated.

Goldman appeared in the living room with a bag in his hand. "I found an article of clothing on your fence, Mr. Grunch. Can you identify it?"

"That doesn't belong to me or to the Mrs., detective," maintained Mr. Grunch.

"We'll have to take it down to the lab and have it checked," Rozas confirmed.

"You sure you're OK?" Detective Goldman asked. "We can call the paramedics. It might be wise to have them take a look. Just in case."

"No, on with you, detective," Mr. Grunch assured him. "Both my wife and I are fine now. We don't need any of those paramedic people. I just hope you gumshoes can track down the culprit who stole my life's treasures."

"We'll be going, then," replied the detective. "We can see ourselves out. Thank you both for your cooperation. Call us if you think of anything. And keep that front door of yours locked. We'll let you know if we get any leads."

On their way to the door, Sid whispered boldly, "Detective Rozas, I think I know someone who looks like the man Mr. Grunch was describing."

Sam frowned and took a step back. He wasn't sure Sid should tell about Kim's cousin.

"He's my friend Kim Chung's cousin, Kenneth, and he's 19," Sid went on. "He's from East Oldham, and he has a scar on his cheek that looks like the one Mr. Grunch described."

Detective Rozas thanked Sid. "I'll get back to you, son, after we've checked it. You're brave."

Mrs. Grunch had prepared some iced tea. "Do you boys prefer lemon or sugar?" she asked, entering the living room with a silver tray.

Hi spoke up. "First, I have something for Mr. Grunch from everyone at Lake School."

As Hi handed the certificate to Mr. Grunch, the old man's voice cracked. "I thank you, lad. It's a real special document and one I will treasure."

"More than that," Mr. Grunch went on, "Without you boys, no telling when we would have been found, and we couldn't have gotten out of those bindings alone. We are grateful to you."

It was the first time the boys had ever seen Mr. Grunch smile. All of their friends had always thought that the Grunches were just two grouchy old people. "Gosh, Mrs. Grunch," Hi

commented, "you're real nice. How come nobody knew?"

Sid North turned his head. His little brother was always saying things that embarrassed him. "Hi didn't mean anything by that," Sid blubbered.

"I know very well what he means. He means a compliment. And I mean to take it that way. I like this boy Hi North." Mrs. Grunch gave Hi a big smile. "Where did you get such a name?"

"When Hi was just a baby," explained Sid, "he said 'hi' to everybody. Mom just started calling him Hi. Pretty soon, he thought it was his name."

Everybody was still chuckling when the three boys hopped aboard their bikes and began pedaling back up the hill toward the North home. Mrs. North was flabbergasted. When Sid explained about Kenneth, she became concerned. "I hope you made the right decision."

"Don't worry, Mom," Sid replied. Jokingly, as the boys left, he added, "You need to switch your radio from that old-time rock and roll to rap, Mom! We're going out to shoot some baskets."

"I'll rap you if you don't get on out of here and use up some of that energy of yours," Mrs. North warned. "Go on now. I need to finish my work."

It was hot for spring. The glare from the sun was so bright that by 3:30, Sam and Sid decided to quit. They had just slumped onto the kitchen chairs, hot and exhausted, when the red telephone on the counter began to ring. Sam looked at Sid. "I hope it's not who I think it is, Buddy."

When he hung up, Sid had to recount Detective Rozas' message to Sam, his mom, and Hi, who were eager to hear what had happened.

"He told me they had questioned Kim's cousin, Kenneth," confided Sid. "Kenneth's in the clear. He was with Kim and her mom at the zoo this morning."

"So how do you feel about ratting now?" inquired Sam.

"Well, actually, Detective Rozas said that if everybody told what they knew, we could virtually eliminate crime. We'd all be safe. Anyway," Sid went on, "they found the real crook. A call came in from South Street from another couple this afternoon. Attempted robbery. But this time the old gent was a retired policeman and he caught the crook red-handed!"

Mrs. North's old time rock and roll radio station interrupted them with the hourly news:

"This just in. The Jasper Police Department confirms that William Smolder, age 21, has just been arrested for the recent burglary spree involving senior citizens. The police have recovered all of the stolen articles in Mr. Smolder's van . . . ."

Vocabulary Expansion

Describe and define these words and phrases:

certificate of appreciation	flabbergasted	motivate
gives me the creeps	ajar	vacillate
promenade	gain back strength	trespasser
evidence	life savings	look-alike
in the clear	rock and roll	rap
right decision	"Sold" sign	askew
wraparound porch	bound and gagged	hoarse
document	philanthropy	

Language Expansion Activities

1. Make an appointment with a police officer. Many times officers will visit schools to talk with students. Ask the officer about how he or she tracks down evidence. Ask him or her to explain how important it is for people to tell the police everything they know concerning any criminal act. Discuss the police officer's comments with your group. Then write a paragraph about your feelings toward what the officer told you.

2. Write a paragraph about the interview Detectives Rozas and Goldman had with Kenneth Chung. Be sure to include the types of questions you think they might have asked Kenneth to determine whether or not he had an alibi.

Language Expansion Questions

1. Why did Hi have to go over to Mr. Grunch's house on a beautiful Saturday morning? Why did he protest?

2. What did Sam and Sid have to postpone so that they could go with Hi? Would your older sibling postpone his/her Saturday activities to accompany you anywhere? Would you?

3. Tell how Mr. and Mrs. Grunch were feeling when they were finally rescued. Discuss their feelings.

4. Identify an event in the story that you would not like to have happen to you. Identify one that you wish would happen.

5. Retell the story, having the boys find Mr. and Mrs. Grunch happily sitting on their porch when they arrive. Would this version of the story have been better or worse? Tell why.

6. Sid was hesitant about telling the police about Kim's cousin. Why did he feel that way? Have you ever had to tell on someone? Was it the right thing to do?

7. Write a description of the two detectives.

8. What are some of the advantages and disadvantages of becoming a senior citizen? Write and discuss your findings.

9. What if the boys hadn't come along when they did? How do you think Mr. and Mrs. Grunch would have been rescued?

10. With your group, play the roles of senior citizens. What did it teach you?

Unit 44

AN OVERSIGHT

UNIT 44

Phonology/Orthography Concepts

- Phonograms are letter groups that usually represent the same sounds (phonemes).
- The phonogram **igh** represents the long /i/ phoneme.

Vocabulary

blight	high	right	*door*
bright	light	sigh	*laugh*
fight	might	sight	*often*
flight	night	slight	
fright	plight	tight	

AN OVERSIGHT

Story Summary:

When an injustice has been done, the friends discover what it means to fight city hall. Kim Chung leads the forces of rebellion against the city council.

A month ago, when Kim Chung had decided to fight city hall, she had been alone. Then Tam Turner, Pat Marks, and Molly Manchester had agreed to help. Before it was over, more than twenty students from their school were working on the project. They needed 2,500 signatures to overturn the city council's decision. At the end of the city council meeting last Monday night, it seemed there was no chance of winning the fight Kim had begun.

Kim had first discussed the problem in history class. "The city council has voted to permit some company to build a chemical waste disposal plant in Jasper. We don't know what pollution problems this might create! Nobody has investigated this company. We don't know what happened in other towns where they have chemical waste disposal plants!" Kim Chung was usually a little reserved. But on the issue of pollution, she was very concerned. She wanted her classmates' help.

Yesterday, Mr. Wood had told his history class, "In light of the fact that the vote has already taken place, I'm not sure you can do anything, but I'll try to find out the right way to approach this."

Today, Mr. Wood had returned to class with the information they needed. "Overturning a vote of the city council," he told them, "requires a petition with 2,500 signatures. Once that petition is completed, you can request an open vote by the entire city. That would permit enough time for the citizens to investigate the company's record."

"Mr. Wood," Kim asserted, "I would like to use this for my Social Studies Fair project. I know the Fair isn't until next semester, but if I begin working on it now, I could have my report finished by then. It's just that I'm going to need some help."

"Nobody's going to pay attention to some girl knocking on their door talking about pollution!" Nick Hopkins retorted. "What a sight!"

"Removing a Blight On the City! That could be the title of your report!" Al Long and Mat Miller were laughing so hard that Mr. Wood had to scold them.

"Kim's idea is a good one," he said, "and I will accept it as her Social Studies Fair project. Too often, citizens let things happen to them. Too often, people don't do or say anything about the problems they see in their community. What happens then?"

"People suffer the consequences! Kim's right!" Pat Marks defended her friend. After school that day, some of the girls in the class agreed to meet that night at Pat's house to plan the petition drive.

"Just to show them," Tam Turner suggested, "I think Kim *ought* to call her project 'Removing a Blight.' Wait 'til Kim wins the state Social Studies Fair. Then they'll stop laughing about what one girl can do!"

"I've been thinking," Kim announced when four girls from Mr. Wood's history class met at Pat's house that night. "What would be the best thing we could do to protect our city? If we all worked together, we could make this a group project for the Social Studies Fair. Maybe some adults would help us. Lots of adults are concerned about pollution."

"Right!" Molly interjected. "I already know an adult who will help us. Right after school, I went to Jen Wells' Pet Shop to pick up a new book on Arabian horses. While I was there, Jen was lecturing Sam Webster about the problems that our generation might face if we don't try to do something about this chemical waste disposal plant!"

"Were any other boys there?" asked Tam.

"Al came in with Mat to get some flea soap," Molly answered. "When the two of them heard what Jen had to say about how big this problem could get, they changed their tune. You know how they all listen to Jen. They even offered to help us."

Jen Wells owned a pet shop down at the dock, near Chick's Fish Shack, which was owned and operated by Mat's father. In the summer and on holidays, the kids had spent many happy hours at the dock. Chick would give them scraps to feed the seagulls. Sometimes a ship captain would let them come aboard. Sam helped out at Jen's Pet Shop. Once, when Ted had been in the hospital, the kids had operated his Shell Shop, under Jen's supervision. The dock was like a second home to them.

"What if we call Jen and ask her how to begin?" Tam offered. "She'll help us. Maybe she knows somebody on the city council."

"Tam's right," Pat agreed. "Let's call Jen."

Just then, Pat's father opened the door of her room, where the girls were meeting. "Trish and I are going to get some frozen yogurt. Anybody else interested?" he asked.

"Oh, Dad!" Pat implored, "Could you please bring us some Chocolate Delight? It's a new nonfat, no-sugar flavor. And Dad, do you know anybody on the city council?"

Herbert Marks was always fascinated by his daughter and her friends. What in the world could Chocolate Delight yogurt have to do with the city council? "What are you kids up to this time?" he asked. "It seems like every time you have a project, my daughter manages to get *me* involved! Yes, I know some people on the city council. Yes, I'll get you some Chocolate Delight. Now Trish and I are leaving before I get roped into another one of your projects!" Herbert Marks laughed.

By Saturday, the four girls had met with Jen Wells and had organized teams of students from Mr. Wood's history class to cover the entire city limits. Each team had a petition form which Jen had created on her computer.

"When they open the door," Jen had advised them, "be polite. Just ask them if they know about the vote of the city council. Ask whether they want a chemical waste disposal plant here in Jasper. Ask the person to sign the petition if they think the entire city should vote. Be sure they understand that this is the only legal way to overturn the vote of the city council."

Kim and Pat took one side of Newtown Avenue, and Tam and Molly knocked on doors on the other side of the street. People were interested. Nearly everyone they asked signed their petition.

Sam Webster had agreed to lead another team of petitioning students in the area around the dock. The students were advised that some people might not talk to them. But high spirits rose higher as they went from door to door, explaining the problem. People *were* interested. Very few refused to sign.

Sam and Kim had instructed the others to meet back at Jen Wells' Pet Shop at 3:00 that afternoon. Jen helped them with the count. By that evening, they realized that they had a total of 3,488 signatures! Now, all they had to do was take their petition to the city council meeting on Monday night!

Entering the city council chamber, the students  were accompanied by their teacher, Mr. Wood, Jen Wells, and some of their parents. It was very noisy. Some people from the TV station waited with their minicams for the meeting to begin. City council members began to take their assigned seats.

Mat Miller's parents were there. They knew what a chemical waste disposal plant could do to their business. They owned Chick's Fish Shack, where they sold all kinds of seafood. If chemicals got into the water, the seafood would be poisoned.

The president of the city council was a woman named Barbara Baylor. She banged her gavel, opened the meeting, and announced the night's agenda. Kim's petition was not announced as an item to be discussed.

"Excuse me, Madam President," Kim pleaded. "I object. I have a petition to be

announced. I turned it in yesterday. Why isn't it on the agenda?"

"Who is this girl?" Ms. Baylor shouted. "Clerk! Advise visitors to the city council chambers that children under 21 years old are not allowed to participate in the business of the city council. Let's get back to the meeting."

The meeting continued until 9:30. As they left, Kim felt dejected. After all this work, after she had gotten so many friends involved in her project, Ms. Baylor had refused to hear her petition. "I just don't understand, Mom," she sighed. "It seems so unfair. So many people signed the petition."

"You're right, Kim," Doris Chung reassured her daughter. "It isn't fair. And I'm going to see what we can do about it."

As they neared the parking lot, they saw Jen Wells talking to Chick and Pam Miller and Herbert Marks. They were all angry. "That woman has completely ignored the wishes of the people," Herbert Marks asserted. "Kim may have started the petition, but the voters of this city signed it. We're not going to let this issue die."

"I have an idea, Herb," Mr. Wood offered. "We might be in

for a fight, but it's worth it." They agreed to meet at Pam and Chick Miller's house for coffee and to discuss Mr. Wood's plan.

Mr. and Mrs. Webster were there with their son, Sam. Sam had worked as hard as Kim. Everybody understood what this petition meant—not just to the kids, but to the city. "We'll be there as soon as we take Sam home, Chick," Mr. Webster said.

"Bring Sam with you," replied Chick. "These kids did all the footwork. They should be involved!"

A year ago, Pam and Chick Miller had bought a huge old house—a fixer-upper near the dock, and they had worked hard on it. Lightposts lit the front of the house, and in the chilly autumn evening, their home was bright and beautiful. As they got out of their car, the two stood and admired their work. Chick said, "I'm sorry Mat stayed home tonight with Joy. He should have been at that meeting, too."

Inside, Mat had just gotten Joy to sleep when he heard his dad's hatchback pull up in the driveway. Joy was the Millers' baby daughter, who was just over a year old. It seemed to Mat that whenever his parents were at home, Joy was just fine. But whenever Mat was baby-sitting, she wanted to stay up and play all night. He pulled the draperies aside, and saw cars pulling up all around

their house. "What in the world is going on?" Mat wondered to himself.

"Hi, Honey," Pam said as she rushed by Mat on her way to the kitchen. "Chick, where is that big coffee urn that makes 24 cups? Is it in the garage?"

"I don't know about the rest of you, but I was outdone by the way Ms. Baylor ramrodded that meeting tonight," began Jen Wells.

"Evidently the plight of this city is not her first concern," added Frank Wood, the history teacher. "She was elected to represent all of the people. She must have forgotten that fact."

"There is another fact that I discovered today when I was down at city hall on business," Herbert Marks interjected. "It seems that Ms. Baylor owns a great deal of stock in the company that wants to build this chemical waste disposal plant. I think that there is a way to get her to put that petition on the city council meeting agenda next week."

The adults sat around planning their strategy, and by 11:00 they had reached an agreement. Jen Wells and Herbert Marks would make the appointment to meet with Ms. Baylor. The others would encourage everyone they knew to attend the city council meeting next Monday.

"You know," Mr. Wood commented, as he and Jen left, "this is a great way for our kids to learn about how democracy works!"

The next Monday night, Ms. Baylor began once more with a bang of the gavel. But the meeting took a different turn this time. "It seems there was an *oversight* last Monday," she began. "We're ready to hear the petition. This time it is being brought forth by registered voters." Within ten minutes, an open vote of the people had been scheduled. The citizens would make their own decision about what would happen in their city.

That night, when Kim and her mother sat on Kim's bed remembering the whole thing, Kim said, "Last week I didn't believe there was a chance. Mom, isn't it amazing how you can feel so desolate, and then a week later be on top of the world?"

Doris Chung gave her daughter a big hug. "You'll never know how proud I am of you!"

Vocabulary Expansion

Describe and define these words and phrases:

remove the blight	fight city hall	suffer the consequences
in light of the fact	sign a petition	overturn a vote
changed their tune	get roped into	chemical waste disposal plant
like a second home	assigned seats	just over a year old
under supervision	an oversight	what in the world
a little reserved	cars pulling up	own stock in a company
do the footwork	registered voter	took a different turn
bang the gavel		on top of the world

Language Expansion Activities

1. Identify some of the causes of pollution in your community. Make a list of things that the citizens could do to prevent these problems. Write a report detailing the ways that pollution could be prevented in your community. Discuss these possibilities with your group. What are the advantages of each possibility? What are the disadvantages?

2. Take a poll of twenty voters. Find out: (1) what they think is the major source of pollution in your community; and (2) what solution they think should be provided. Next, combine your findings with those of your group. Make a list of the voters' concerns, with the number of persons who identified each one. Then, list the pollution concerns in order of severity, as identified by the voters. Send your list to your city council or mayor.

Language Expansion Questions

1. What was the problem that caused Kim to begin the project?

2. Explain how Kim's project became a school project.

3. Why did Ms. Baylor *say* she refused to accept the students' petition? What was her *real* reason? What changed her mind?

4. At first, some of the boys in the class laughed at Kim's idea. Why? Has anybody ever laughed when you were serious about something? How did you feel?

5. How many voters' signatures on a petition did they need to overturn the city council's vote? How many votes did they actually get? How many extra signatures did they have?

6. Why was it important to have the entire city involved, instead of just the city council?

7. What does a chemical waste disposal plant do? Are such plants necessary? Do you think anybody really wants them in their own city? If you were the President, how would you solve this problem?

8. How did Herbert Marks feel about his daughter, Pat, and her friends? Support your position with text from the story.

9. In the dictionary, look up the meaning of *democracy*. Explain how the events in this story describe the workings of a democratic form of government.

10. Is there a problem in your town or city that causes concern for the citizens? What are the citizens doing about it? What *could* they do about it that would help to solve the problem?

Unit 45

NOTHING VENTURED, NOTHING GAINED

UNIT 45

Phonology/Orthography Concepts

- Phonograms are letter groups that usually represent the same sounds (phonemes).
- In the phonogram **ind**, **i** represents the long /i/ phoneme.
- The phonogram **ture** represents the sound pattern /chur/.

Vocabulary

behind	grind	rapture	*fought*
bind	kind	remind	*ocean*
blind	lecture	rewind	
capture	mankind	rind	
couture	mature	rupture	
culture	mind	stature	
denture	mixture	suture	
feature	moisture	texture	
find	nature	torture	
fixture	nurture	unkind	
fracture	overwind	venture	
furniture	pasture	vulture	
future	picture	wind	
gesture	posture		

NOTHING VENTURED, NOTHING GAINED

Story Summary:

Al gets a job helping out at the bookstore. He finds out that the store owner, Mr. Pasture, needs more help than just cleaning up. Al helps Mr. Pasture modernize his store's operations.

"Come on, Mom," Al pleaded. "I'll do anything to get a computer. Can't you just give me a loan on my allowance?"

"Like maybe 50 years in advance?" Mrs. Long said, teasing her son. "Honey," she went on, "we just can't afford to buy you a new computer. Why don't you go downtown and see if you can get a job helping out at one of the stores? Maybe you could do odd jobs or run errands. If you want to get a new computer, you're going to have to earn the money."

"Fat chance anybody downtown would want to help out a kid," Al muttered under his breath. But he grabbed his jacket and a rice cake for the road.

It felt like spring. No buds on the trees yet, but Al would have preferred anything to working indoors today. He had spring fever. "I have to be mature about this," he thought to himself.

Inside the health food store, the lady at the counter spoke. "May I help you?" she asked.

"I wondered. Are there any jobs I could do for you?" Al bid. "I need to earn some money."

"I'm sorry," the kind lady said. "I'd really like to help you. Try us again next summer. We just don't have anything at the moment."

Al wouldn't give up. "Do you know of any stores in the area who are looking for somebody to do odd jobs?" he added.

"You might try over at the bookstore," she responded. "Mr. Pasture is all by himself. Books are heavy and he could probably use a strong healthy fellow to help stock the shelves. By the way, he loves books, but he's a little absentminded. I ordered some books from him: After they arrived, he never sent me a bill. And just between the two of us," she added with a whisper, "that old store could use a good cleaning. There's plenty of opportunity to help Mr. Pasture. I know he sells a lot of books."

"Thanks a lot for the tip," Al called out as he left. He walked down the street toward the bookstore. The place looked old and run-down. "I hope it's not as bad as it looks," Al thought.

As Al approached the bookstore, he saw Mr. Pasture through the window. "He kind of looks like

Albert Einstein," Al said to himself, smiling, "same gestures, too."

Opening the door to the bookstore, Al noticed that Mr. Pasture seemed to have the same sort of personality he'd imagined for Einstein as well. Albert Einstein was Al's hero. His friends thought Al reminded *them* of Albert Einstein. "Now, where did I put that first edition copy of Dickens?" Mr. Pasture was mumbling to himself. He didn't even see Al coming in.

The clerk at the health food store was right. It was a good thing Al didn't have an allergy to dust. He would have sneezed himself right out the door and into the street!

"Sir," Al said. Old Mr. Pasture didn't even look up. "I'll bet he's hard of hearing, too," Al thought. "Sir!" he said louder with a cough, still trying to be polite. "Excuse me, sir!" he shouted.

"Yes, young man," replied Mr. Pasture with a smile. "What can I do for you? Let's see, you look like the studious type.

History, geography, science? Science it is! I'll bet my last nickel!"

"You're right about that, sir," Al replied. "I love science. Especially computer science! But that's not why I'm here right now," Al added hopefully. "I really need a part-time job. I can clean, dust, move books, stock shelves, file . . . ."

"Hold on there a minute, young man," Mr. Pasture stopped him. "Why would you think I might be needin' any help around here?"

"Well," Al answered honestly, "you've got the only bookstore in town. And you're always busy. Maybe too busy to get to some important jobs, like dusting and sweeping for starters. Those windows of yours are pretty gray. I'll bet lots of people walk by and don't even see all the great books you have in your display window. Just picture that window sparkling clean!" Al's voice got a little stronger as he went on. "I could give you a hand with those boxes in the corner, and any deliveries you might have."

"Well, there now. You're just full of good ideas, lad. I like that. What's your name, son?" Mr. Pasture considered as he scratched his head.

"My name is Al Long, sir," Al stated. "And I really do need a job."

"Name's John Pasture," said the old man as he put out his wrinkled hand to shake. "I guess you're right, Mr. Al Long," he added with a grunt. "This old store could use a good cleanin'. Broom's in the closet. Washroom's in the rear. Get yourself an apron and go to it."

Al hesitated for a moment. "Excuse me, sir. I'm glad to have the job. But what's my pay?"

"When I was your age, I got paid a dime an hour," Mr. Pasture said. "But, of course times have changed. I'll start you at minimum wage."

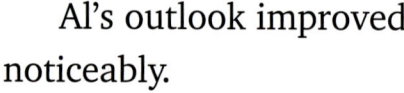

Al's outlook improved noticeably.

"And," Mr. Pasture continued, "if you work out, I'll do even better. I like a hard worker who's always looking to improve."

Al shook Mr. Pasture's hand and quickly went to find an apron. He fought his way through the clutter to start cleaning, washing, and polishing. Within hours, the place sparkled. Sunlight poured in the display windows. Half-empty boxes that had lined the aisles were gone, and the shelves were filled with stock.

When Al looked around, he realized what a great store it was. Mr. Pasture had some really wonderful old books—and hundreds that Al had never seen before. As Al worked, several customers came into the store to buy books or just to chat with Mr. Pasture.

Many customers were old friends. "John, what a difference in your store. I don't mind browsin' for a while," Ted, the old sailor, declared. "Cleaner 'n any ship's deck on an ocean voyage!"

"I've had some help here this morning from this young lad, Al Long," Mr. Pasture noted.

"Al's a friend of mine," Ted confided to Mr. Pasture. "Known the lad since he was a toddler. Good family, too. How ya' doin,'  lad?" Ted called out to Al, who was lifting books onto shelves.

"Just great, Ted," shouted Al. "See you down at the dock sometime, Ted!"

Just then, an austere woman with an unkind disposition captured Mr. Pasture's attention. "I got this bill in the mail this morning," she announced as she tapped Mr. Pasture on the shoulder, "and I'm very angry. These aren't the books I bought! *I didn't buy any of these books!*" She was demanding satisfaction.

"Let's see that bill, Mrs. Suskind," Mr. Pasture replied apologetically, lifting his glasses. Al noticed moisture on Mr. Pasture's brow.

Mr. Pasture sat at an old-fashioned rolltop desk that was piled with papers, and gestured for Al to help with other customers at the checkout counter. While Al waited behind the counter, an irate Mrs. Suskind kept tapping her toe, her face turning redder and redder. She watched as Mr. Pasture pawed through a pile of papers.

"Well, I never!" Al heard her mutter under her breath. The minutes crawled.

"Mind if I help you look for that bill, Mr. Pasture?" Al asked with a smile. He could tell that Mr. Pasture had reached his saturation point.

"That would be great, Al," Mr. Pasture sighed. "I know Mrs. Suskind's records are in this pile. I keep all my bills right here in this old rolltop of mine."

Al stared at the collection of papers. There was no way to tell which bills were paid and which were unpaid.

All the bills were clumped together in a single wad and

held with a rubber band. "No wonder this customer got the wrong bill," Al thought.

Mr. Pasture approached another customer who had been waiting while Al found the bill. After she paid it, Mrs. Suskind left in a huff. She had bought three books, but not the three she was charged for.

Later, just before closing time, Mr. Pasture and Al had a long conversation. Mr. Pasture confided that he loved books and could sell them all day, but he'd always had trouble with the "business end" of the bookstore. "Too many back orders. Too many bills. Sometimes I think I'd just rather give the books away than go through all that!" Mr. Pasture gasped.

"What you need is a computer!" Al asserted.

"You can't teach an old dog new tricks," the old man groaned. "I'm too old for computers!"

At dinner that evening, Al said to his parents, "I know a computer would help. Mr. Pasture's just disorganized."

"It's not appropriate for you to interfere in the business, Al," his mother contended.

"He said I could come back tomorrow!"

"Not tomorrow, Al. You've got a big history test on Friday and you need to study. I'm not going to let you ruin your grades over this job."

"But, Mom . . . . "

"Don't 'but mom' me," declared Mrs. Long.

The week dragged. When Al returned to the bookstore Friday afternoon, he explained, "Mom wouldn't let me come back to work until my studies were done."

"Your mother's right," Mr. Pasture agreed. "School should always come first."

The cash register rang and rang all that afternoon. Big orders kept coming in. "Your new window display of best-sellers is working like magic," Mr. Pasture told Al.

"Thanks, sir," Al expressed with a grin. He had never felt quite so appreciated.

On Saturday morning, Al stopped by the computer store. "I feel like I must do something for Mr. Pasture," Al thought to himself. "After all, he gave me a break. I just have to find a way to help him."

Al talked to the store owner, Mr. Grinder, and together they went to see Mr. Pasture.

Mr. Grinder showed Mr. Pasture a computer and a software package that could help him solve many of his problems. Mr. Grinder gave Mr. Pasture brochures and explained the basics of the computer's system operations to him.

"But I don't even know how to turn the darn thing on," Mr. Pasture maintained. Convincing him just to try it was not going to be easy. In fact, it seemed fairly impossible.

"I'll be glad to show you all the basics, Mr. Pasture," Al urged. "Once you get the hang of it, I just know you'll love what it can do for you."

"And you can use it for the first 30 days free," Mr. Grinder offered. "If it doesn't work out for you, I'll take it back. No charge."

"Well," said Mr. Pasture scratching his head, "Nothing ventured, nothing gained. Right, Al?"

"Right on, Mr. Pasture," Al blurted out.

Later that afternoon, the machine was installed. Al started typing files and printing updated bills. He worked all day Sunday, too. Mr. Pasture mailed the bills on Monday morning.

Al didn't get back to the store until Friday.

"Welcome, lad," Mr. Pasture greeted Al. "This new computer is sure efficient. I've been typing in the day's receipts, just like you showed me. But it hasn't made a lick of money for me yet!"

Just then, Mrs. Suskind walked in and plunked down a check for $125.00. "Well, I see you finally got a new billing system," she asserted. "It's about time you billed me for that dictionary I bought last May. Glad to pay my bills on time." She stepped out of the store on the heels of the mail carrier. The mail carrier set down a stack of envelopes, filled with checks for payment.

Mr. Pasture was sitting on top of the world. Al Long had escorted him into the Twenty-First Century! And he loved being in it!

Vocabulary Expansion

Describe and define these words and phrases:

nothing ventured, nothing gained
demanding satisfaction
teach an old dog new tricks
software package
times have changed
potential customer
full of stock
business end
best-seller
sitting on top of the world

health food
absentminded
computer science
compiling data
Albert Einstein
fat chance
pawed through
need a miracle
benefactor
Twenty-First Century

Language Expansion Activities

1. Have a debate with a student or teacher. One of you take Mr. Pasture's side: *Computers are too complicated to do me any good.* And one of you take sides with Al and Mr. Grinder: *Computers can help make your business more efficient.* Before you begin your debate, prepare by making a list of points for each side.

2. Make use of the illustrations in this book to help you design a perfect bookstore. List at least ten books you would want on the shelves of your perfect bookstore. Would you want small couches and chairs for children and large reading chairs for adults? Think about what you would include. Share your design with the others in your group.

Language Expansion Questions

1. Why did Al need a part-time job?

2. Where did he go first to look for a job?

3. Explain how Al convinced Mr. Pasture to give him a job.

4. Identify those activities Al had to do at the bookstore. Would you want to do those things instead of what you normally do after school and on weekends? For money?

5. Change the story so that Mr. Pasture rejects the idea of the computer. Write a new ending for the story.

6. Al wanted to help Mr. Pasture because he had given Al a chance. Is there anyone who has given you a chance at anything? Write about that person.

7. Pretend you are a salesperson at the bookstore. How would you persuade someone to buy a certain book?

8. Offer two reasons why you think Mr. Pasture finally decided to give the computer a try. Name something that you had to be *convinced* to try.

9. Al's mom told him to stay out of Mr. Pasture's affairs. Judge whether Al made the right decision.

10. Al said that his hero was Albert Einstein. Do you have a hero? If not, select one and write about him/her. Share with your group your reasons for selecting the person you did.

Unit 46

THE WEIGHT OF THE WORLD

UNIT 46

Phonology/Orthography Concepts

- Phonograms are letter groups that usually represent the same sounds (phonemes).
- The phonogram **eigh** represents the long /a/ phoneme.

Vocabulary

eight	neigh	sleighride	*love*
eighteen	neighbor	weigh	
eighth	neighborhood	weight	
eighty	neighboring		
freight	sleigh		

THE WEIGHT OF THE WORLD

Story Summary:

No matter how hard she tries, Pat Marks has terrible difficulty with math. While Kim tries to provide her friend Pat with moral support, she discovers that there are huge problems in her own family.

As far as Pat Marks was concerned, eighth grade was about the worst thing she had ever experienced. It seemed like there were too many classes, too many assignments, too many rules, too many teachers. "I'd love to be back in elementary school," she confided to Kim Chung, who had been her best friend and her neighbor since kindergarten. "All this stuff just weighs heavy on my mind. Seems like there's no time for fun anymore."

Kim shrugged her shoulders. "It seems about the same to me," she countered. "You just had a bad day, that's all."

"Kim, you don't know what it's like to have so much trouble in school. I got eighteen problems wrong on my math test. When my dad sees this paper, you'll be able to hear him all over the neighborhood." Pat was more upset than Kim could ever remember.

The two friends slammed their lockers and snaked down the hall. On Friday afternoons, students were always rushing to get somewhere. It was like a gigantic traffic jam composed of humans. Several students spoke to Pat, but she didn't answer anybody.

"You don't have to be so stuck up, Pat Marks!" A seventh grader she hardly knew was shouting at her. The girl walked off in a huff.

"Don't think anything of that, Pat," reassured Kim. "Sometimes when people have problems, other people take it personally. She'll get over it. I know you're not stuck up."

When they got outdoors, they realized it had gotten colder. "See what I mean?" Pat contended. "Even the weather's turned sour. Last week we thought spring was here, and now it's like midwinter again. The temperature's probably dropped twenty degrees. All I brought to school was this sweater. We'll probably freeze to death walking home!" Pat was in a dark mood. The weight of her schoolbooks was a heavy burden.

"I wish I didn't have to go to school. I wish there was no such thing as math. I'm sick of it!" Kim had tried to help her, but Pat had trouble with math.

Sid North and Sam Webster called to the girls from behind. "Pat! Kim!"

"What do *they* want?" Pat grumbled disagreeably.

Sam was insistent. "Hey, you two! Everybody's going skating tonight. It's two for one. If one person pays, the other person gets in free. Wanna go?"

"We're going," Sid said. "Everybody's going. Like, are you two going or what?"

"Sid makes me so mad," Pat commented to Kim. "Ever since he won King of the Rink that night two years ago, he acts like he's some kind of skating champion or something. He's not even that good of a skater."

"Hey, guys," Kim said as the two caught up with the girls from behind. "Pat had a bad day. Math again."

"Why didn't you call me, Pat?" Sid asked. "I told you if you needed help with math I'd help you. It's easy enough to pick up the telephone."

Pat's head felt like it was going to burst. All the frustration she felt inside emerged in a screaming rage. "You just love making fun of me, don't you? All of you! All three of you think you're so smart because you always understand math and I never do. Well, I'm sick of it. I'm sick of all of you. Just leave me alone!"

Pat Marks dashed into the street, and into the traffic. Horns were blaring. People were shouting at her. She didn't hear a thing. By the time she reached the edge of her own neighborhood, she couldn't even remember how she had gotten there. "Dad doesn't understand," she mumbled to herself. "The last time I brought home an 'F' in math, he said he better never see another one," she remembered. "Even Trish does better than me in math, and she's only in the third grade!"

Tears flooded her face. The weight of the world was on her shoulders. For the first time in her life, Pat Marks was thinking about running away. As she turned onto the walkway to the front door, her father drove into the driveway. "Pat!" he shouted. "Pat! Where's your coat? It's freezing out! I told you when you left this morning to take your coat because the temperature was going to drop. Pat! What's wrong with you?" Herbert Marks sat in his car and watched as his daughter ignored him, stormed through the front door, and slammed it behind her.

Pat's father grabbed his briefcase and dashed up the walkway. He didn't even take the time to put his car in the garage. He was angry. Pat was in the eighth grade now, and she should be acting more grown-up, not less. It had reached the point that he could count on Trish more than Pat, and Trish was only eight years old.

Herb had had a bad day at work. His secretary had told him that she was moving away. His best customer had canceled. And now he had to come home to this. "That girl doesn't appreciate a single thing I do for her," he grumbled to himself. "Pat thinks the world revolves around her, but she's got another think coming!" Herbert Marks slammed the door behind him.

Sometimes, he thought, life was just too difficult. His wife, the girls' mother, had died when the girls were very young. Herb had tried his best to be both father and mother to his daughters. But life had a way of dropping problems at his doorstep—no matter how hard he tried. Last year, his father had died. Now his mother was living alone on the family farm in Wisconsin. Herb worried about his mom every day, trying to run a farm with only a hired man.

Sometimes Herb wanted to throw in the towel. But he kept on going. Now he remembered a poem he'd learned in eighth grade; how had it gone? "Life won't be a crystal stair?" He tried to remember. Herb decided to look it up—after he'd talked with Pat.

When Kim Chung arrived home, her cousin, Kenneth, dozed on the living room couch. Kenneth had graduated from high school last year, and he didn't have a job. Kenneth had arrived last Friday, announcing to Kim and her mom that he would "spend a few days with you until I can find a job in Jasper."

So far as Kim could tell, Kenneth had not done a single thing to look for a job. He had managed to eat all the food in the refrigerator and all the food in the pantry—but he had contributed nothing.

"Hey, hey, li'l cuz; what's happenin'?" Kenneth's sleepy greeting fell on deaf ears. Kim went into her room and locked the door. "I'll just stay here until Mom gets home from school," she thought.

Kim's mom, Doris, was a teacher. She and Kim had been alone for several years now, a family of two. Doris Chung had been solely responsible for bringing up her daughter. Being a single parent was difficult, but Doris did her best. "I wonder what

Mom will say when she gets home and finds Kenneth still here," Kim mused. "He was supposed to have been here for three days. Today's Friday. It's been a week." Kim pulled her history book from her backpack. She would get her homework finished and feel free the entire weekend.

    Herbert sat down in the living room. He needed some time to think before he talked to Pat. The sky was darker now. Could snow be on its way this late in the year? Just a week ago, everybody had thought spring was here. Now, looking out the French doors onto his back patio, Herb noted a bleak, threatening sky and the shrill shrieking of a north wind. His heart was heavy.

    When he had first moved into this neighborhood, Pat had been in kindergarten, and Trish was not quite a year old. It had been just after his wife died. He had wanted to create a fresh start for himself and for his girls. Herb had decided to move into the new house because living in the old one—where they had been so happy—was painful for him. He saw his wife around every corner. But now she was gone.

    Now Pat was thirteen years old, an eighth grader. Before he knew it, he would be packing her off to college. "I wish you were here," he said in a private moment of meditation. "Pat's miserable. At times like these, I know she needs you. There's just no way that a man can be a mother to a girl." Herbert Marks felt his eyes welling with tears. Sorrow drenched his heart.

"Herb! Herb!" Someone was rapping on the window of the kitchen, to the left of the French doors. He hadn't even heard. When he got up to see who it was, he immediately recognized Doris Chung.

"What's going on, Doris?" he asked, opening the French doors. "Is it going to snow, or what? Isn't this weather something?"

"What's going on with you?" Doris asked her neighbor. "I've been banging on the front door and nobody answered. Didn't you hear me? I saw your car in the front drive and decided to try back here."

"Sorry. Guess I've been deep in thought. Or deep in the past. What can I do for you?"

"I'm not sure you can do anything, Herb. But I had to ask. My nephew, Kenneth, arrived here last Friday and said he was going to look for a job. So far, he hasn't had any luck. Have you heard of any positions available downtown? I'm desperate. It looks like Kenneth's camped out with Kim and me until he gets a job and finds a place of his own."

"I don't know, Doris," Herb responded. "If he can type and file, I could probably use him in my office. My secretary told me today that she was quitting and moving to Dallas with her husband. I'm willing to give him a try. But my office is busy. The work's hard, and the pay's not great. Why don't you send him over to see me?"

Lying on her bed, Pat opened the old family scrapbook that Gram had given her the last time she and Trish had gone to Wisconsin for a visit. There were pictures that went back to before the turn of the century. Her father's family had been the first African American family to own land and run a dairy farm in Wisconsin. They had overcome the odds and become prosperous people by working hard.

Here, on the first page, was a picture of an old-fashioned sleigh, drawn by a horse. The picture  was faded, more brown-and-cream than black-and-white. A woman sat high on a wooden seat holding the reins. You could almost hear the horse's neigh and whinny. The woman was young; she wore a scarf around her head and had on a big winter cape. There was no mistaking it: she looked just like Pat!

"I would love to have lived back then," Pat thought to herself. "Life must have been wonderful. Kids could quit school and work on their family's farm. They didn't have to take math tests on Friday." But the woman in the picture kept commanding Pat's attention. "She looks like me! I wonder who this is. I wonder if Dad knows who this is."

Pat picked up the fragile old scrapbook and took it into the kitchen, where she heard her father turning on the faucet. "Dad! Dad! Look at this picture. Look at this lady. She looks just like me! Like, I mean, she looks *exactly* like me, Dad. Do you know who this is?"

"I hope nobody looks like you." A small voice preceded the eight-year old Trish Marks, entering the kitchen. "I got to feel sorry for them if they look like you. They got to be pretty ugly. What's for dinner, Dad?" Trish inquired with an impish grin.

"Trish, where have you been? It's nearly 5:30. You should have been home nearly two hours ago. No phone call. No message. I've been worried!"

"We had Speech Club meeting after school, Dad. We had to practice for the speech meet coming up in May. Remember?" Trish took off her coat and opened her folder. "I got my math test back today, Dad. Could you please sign it so I can turn it in?" Trish grinned. She always did well in math. "You know what the boys in my class said about me, Dad? They said 'Marks always gets the marks.' Get it? Marks always gets the marks. They meant . . . ."

Her big sister interrupted. "We get it, smarty-pants. Everybody knows how smart you are!"

"How about you, Pat? Did you get your math test back today? Let's get all the school papers signed while I have a pen in my hand," urged Herbert.

"We didn't get our tests back," Pat replied. She closed the scrapbook, the lady in the picture forgotten now, and headed back toward her room.

When the phone rang, it was for Pat. Herbert noticed that whenever Pat talked on the phone now, she always whispered, as though she didn't want him or Trish to hear. Pat covered the receiver with her

hand and implored, "Dad, *everybody's* going skating tonight. Nick's mom is driving the van. She'll stay and drive us home. Can I go? Please?"

"Pat. You know that we had this conversation Monday. You're not going anywhere this weekend. You've got to hit the books. That last report card was nothing to be proud of!" Herbert wasn't in the mood to argue.

"But Dad, I don't have any written homework this weekend," she pleaded. "I finished everything I  had to do, and it's all turned in. Please let me go skating tonight. If you let me, I promise I'll stay home all day tomorrow and Sunday and I'll study the rest of the weekend. You don't even have to drive. Nick's mom is driving. Please, Dad!"

Pat had a way of softening her father up, and it was working once more. "I guess so," Herb responded. "If you're sure you don't have any written homework. But I mean it. Saturday and Sunday, you're hitting the books!"

After Pat had gone, Herb and Trish finished the dinner dishes. Trish sat down on the floor and flipped on the TV. Herb picked up the newspaper to search for his treat of the day: the crossword puzzle. "Trish," he said, "bring your old dad a sharp pencil with a good eraser. I can't write with this thing!"

"I don't have any pencils, Daddy," she replied. "Our teacher makes us write with pens. She said next year we're going to be in fourth, and we have to learn to write with pens." Trish went back to her program.

Herb walked over to the piano bench and picked up Pat's backpack. "There's got to be a pencil in here," he muttered. He removed books and papers, stacking them on the bench. At the bottom, he felt some pencils. As he fished one out, a paper drifted to the floor. Herb couldn't help seeing the teacher's note, written in red block letters: *Pat, Please see me. You got eighteen of thirty-three problems wrong. Your grade on this test was 46–F. Did you study? You'll need to spend some extra time on math this weekend!*

Herbert Marks felt that weight on his shoulders again. Why hadn't Pat asked him to help her? Her friend Sid was an excellent math student who had offered many times to help Pat with math. Where in the world had that girl gotten such a hard head?

He decided that as soon as Pat got home, they would have to have a talk. No more postponement.

He kept looking at the math test and the note the teacher had written. How could Pat have been so deceptive? What was happening to that girl? She had always been such a *good* girl. Why couldn't she tell him the truth? Wasn't he being a good father? Was it his fault?

When the phone rang, Herb picked it up. He didn't really want to talk to anybody. "Herb? Herb, I hate to bother a friend and neighbor on Friday night. But I don't know where else to turn!" Doris Chung's voice was shaking. "Do you think I could come over? I'm alone. Kim went skating."

Doris came in through the French doors, the entrance used by most of the neighborhood. "Herb. Thanks. Do you have any coffee? I don't know what to do. Remember when I was asking about my nephew, Kenneth, this afternoon?"

"Sure, Doris. I said I'd be glad to give him a try at the office, see if it works out." Herb poured some coffee and handed her the mug. "Sit down at the table, Doris. What can I do for you?"

"I know you'll think I'm a fool. I hadn't seen Kenneth Chung for several years, not since he was about eight years old. So when he arrived last

Friday, I just assumed that he was who he said he was.

"Earlier this afternoon I put in a call to his mother, but she wasn't there. I left a message on her answering machine, telling her that Kenneth was still here, and not to worry.

"She just called me back, Herb. Not fifteen minutes ago. She said that Kenneth is at home! This person who is camped out in my house is not even my nephew! And I've left Kim alone with him this week! He's out now. He said he was meeting a man about a job. What am I going to do, Herb?"

"I'll tell you what you're *not* going to do, Doris. You're not going home. We'll call the skating rink and be sure Kim is dropped off here with Pat tonight, instead of at your house. And I'm calling Detective Rozas right now." Herb locked the French doors and drew the draperies.

"You know, Herb," Doris intimated. "Sometimes I feel like I've got the weight of the world on my shoulders. There's so much to do, and so many problems at school, and I worry so much about Kim, and about making ends meet. And now this. Who is this guy? What does he want? How did he get Kenneth's identity? Why us?"

Finally, Herb got a call through to the skating rink. The number there was usually busy. Lucy Hopkins, Nick's mother, had agreed to drop both Kim and Pat at the Marks' home. She would instruct Kim that under no condition was she to go to her own house.

There was good news from Detective Rozas. The man impersonating Kenneth Chung had been arrested during a robbery.

"We've already sent his fingerprints and vital statistics into a computer search," the detective explained to Herb. "It turns out he's wanted in three states for robbery. We got Mr. Grunch coming down here to take a look at him. He might turn out to be the one who robbed the Grunches' house last week. Tell Doris Chung not to worry. This guy's not going anyplace."

"Any idea how he got Kenneth's identity and knew so much about him?" asked Herb. "Doris is concerned, and so is the *real* Kenneth Chung."

"Not yet, but you bet we'll find out before the sky turns light. Tell Mrs. Chung I'll give her a call sometime tomorrow. She can sleep safe. This guy's spending the night with us. He won't be in a comfortable bed tonight!" Detective Rozas was a likable policeman. Everybody respected him. He had been on the police force for several years, and he was a good friend to the people of Jasper.

"Well, I wish our girls would hurry up and get back. As soon as they get here, Kim and I are going home. And we're going to lock the house up tight. And pray for no more long-lost relatives!" Doris and Herb chuckled together, enjoying a last cup of coffee.

But the two of them still carried the weight of the world on their shoulders.

Vocabulary Expansion

Describe and define these words and phrases:

solely responsible	weighs heavy on my mind	stuck up
fell on deaf ears	shrugged her shoulders	in a huff
single parent	the weight of the world	traffic jam
long-lost relative	it had reached the point	French doors
throw in the towel	the world revolves around her	a fresh start
a heavy burden	she's got another think coming	camped out
turn of the century	overcome the odds	impish grin
neigh and whinny	soften her father up	smarty-pants
no comfortable bed	before the sky turns light	two for one
vital statistics	making ends meet	a hard head

Language Expansion Activities

1. Write a biography of the man who impersonated Kenneth Chung. Explain how he got Kenneth's identity, and how he learned of the existence of Kim and Doris Chung. Where did he come from? Tell the story of his life.

2. Pat Marks has serious problems with math. Think of something that has always been difficult for you. Make a list of the things that you have tried to do. Then, write a journal entry discussing people who share this problem: sometimes you can be very good in one thing, but have great difficulty in another area.

Language Expansion Questions

1. Explain the meaning of the title of this story. Why do you think this title was chosen for the story? How many of the characters can you associate with the title?

2. Why didn't Pat show her father the math test? Can you defend what Pat did? Will it be worth it tomorrow? Why?

3. What did Detective Rozas mean when he said, *"He won't be in a comfortable bed tonight!"*?

4. Compare and contrast the lives of Herbert Marks and Doris Chung. How are they alike? How are they different?

5. In this story, the weather seemed to affect people's moods. Do you think the weather affects your moods? Explain how.

6. Why is it important to get to know your neighbors? What things can neighbors do for each other that friends sometimes can't? Think of some specific things that you have done for your neighbors, or that your neighbors have done for you.

7. Pat wished that she had lived at the turn of the century. How would daily life have been different then? Do you think it would really have been better? Explain your reasons.

8. Pat lashed out at her friends after school. How was she feeling? Did Kim take it personally? In what ways was Kim being a good friend? What else might she have done to help Pat?

9. How did Pat feel about her little sister, Trish? Explain the relationship between the two sisters.

10. Discuss Pat's behavior in this story. Does her behavior make Pat a bad person? Decide what you think would be fair treatment. What would you do if you were Herbert Marks?

Unit 47

THE MODERN MEMPHIS

UNIT 47

Phonology/Orthography Concepts

- Phonograms are letter groups that usually represent the same sounds (phonemes).
- The phonogram **ph** represents the phoneme /f/.

Vocabulary

alphabet	Joseph	phony	*rough*
amphibian	Josephson	photograph	*tough*
asphalt	microphone	phrase	
cellophane	neophyte	prophetic	
diphthong	nephew	sapphire	
dolphin	orphan	siphon	
earphones	pamphlet	symphony	
emphasis	Phelps	telephone	
euphoria	phlox	typhoid	
gopher	phone	typhoon	
graph	phoneme	Memphis	
grapheme	phonics		
hyphen	phonograph		

THE MODERN MEMPHIS

Story Summary:

Mat Miller's model riverboat design, *The Modern Memphis*, is chosen for competition in the Mud Island Tenth Anniversary Riverboat Design Contest to be held in Memphis, Tennessee. Mrs. Ranson, the artist in residence at Mat's junior high, accompanies him to Memphis. The trip to Mud Island includes an adventure Mat will never forget. He relearns the importance of being prepared.

The sun's rays danced like tiny fireballs on the wings of the airplane as it circled Memphis International Airport. Mat Miller was excited. He had never flown before and still couldn't believe the circumstances of this flight. He obediently removed his earphones and listened attentively as the flight attendant began:

"Ladies and gentlemen, your airplane is now landing in Memphis. Memphis is Tennessee's biggest city. Memphis is sometimes called the 'Bluff City.' That's because it lies on the Chickasaw Bluffs—or cliffs—next to the Mississippi River.

"Memphis was settled when the prophetic Andrew Jackson and two others bought land here in 1819. They named the town after an ancient Egyptian city, Memphis," he continued.

"Memphis is the world center for buying and selling cotton. One-third of all cotton in the United States is bought and sold each year in Memphis.

"Paper, food products, wooden floors, and electrical equipment are all made in Memphis."

The flight attendant droned on, but Mat was lost in his thoughts. He fidgeted in his seat. Mat knew they were only a few minutes away from landing. Then the excitement he was waiting for would begin.

When the flight attendant mentioned Mud Island, Mat perked up. What he was saying mirrored what Mat had read in the pamphlet Mrs. Ranson had given him. "The Mississippi River, or father of waters, is showcased in every aspect at Mud Island, an actual island in this greatest of American rivers. This is the island's anniversary, the island having been completed in July, 1982. A special celebration at the River Center's exhibit hall this weekend includes model riverboat designs for modern times. You will find many exciting, special events happening there during the entire month of July . . . ."

As the flight attendant continued, Mat whispered to his art teacher and chaperone, Mrs. Ranson, "Just think, Mrs. R., just two months ago I never would have believed this could happen to me. And I owe it all to you! If you hadn't seen a photograph of my computer-powered model riverboat and hadn't known about the contest, we'd never be here."

Mrs. Ranson gave Mat a big smile and continued to listen to the flight attendant.

Mat clung to the arms of his seat as he felt the wheels of the giant aircraft touch down on the asphalt. Although he was trying to listen attentively, Mat couldn't help but be distracted. His ears were popping and his stomach was gurgling with excitement. He had been chosen to accompany the artist in residence from his junior high school, Mrs. Ranson, to the Mud Island Tenth Anniversary Model Riverboat Design Contest. His model, *The Modern Memphis*, had been selected to compete with just nine others in the contest for best model riverboat design. The contest was being held this weekend in the River Museum on Mud Island.

Mat had always loved boats. His father, Chick Miller, owned a fish store at the dock. Since he often helped his dad, Mat had been boarding ships of all sizes, helping to select fish for the store, since he was two. His father also took an interest in boat building. Mat followed suit and had been a neophyte boat builder for years.

Mat remembered vividly his first trip on a riverboat. His grandfather, Leo Kipling, had taken him aboard the River Queen, an Ohio River steamboat, just two summers ago. That trip was indelibly printed into Mat's memory. He had spent much of that trip leaning over the railing of the main deck, observing the Ohio countryside filled with grain elevators, chimneys, and miles and miles of farmland. He remembered a feeling of  euphoria—pure peace—he had experienced on the ride that day.

Mat's grandfather had known the riverboat pilot, and had introduced him to Mat. The pilot had shown Mat the pilot house, several cabins, and the boat's steam engine that turned the paddle wheel. It was during that trip that Mat had been inspired to start building his own model riverboat.

"Mat, we're here!" Mrs. Ranson poked Mat, who had been daydreaming. "It's time to get our bags and get on out to Mud Island," Mrs. Ranson said. "My folks will meet us there later. Mom is volunteering as a guide at the Meditation Gardens at Graceland this month, and Dad has to work until four or so."

"Okay, Mrs. R.," Mat sighed. "I still can't believe we're here. Sure hope I didn't forget anything."

"You had everything when we left this morning!" assured Mrs. Ranson. "Just make sure

 you have your model and your set of blueprints." Mrs. Ranson looked forward to being in Memphis; it was her hometown.

"Right here!" Mat blurted out, opening the overhead luggage compartment and removing a large box and a cardboard packing tube.

As the two rushed toward the baggage claim, Mat remembered, "I promised my friend Nick that I wouldn't leave Memphis without seeing Graceland. He thinks I'll get a glimpse of Elvis Presley's ghost or something. Do you think your mom would give me the tour before we leave town? Really, Mrs. R.," Mat begged, "Nick will kill me if I don't get at least one picture of Graceland."

"Everybody wants to see Graceland," Mrs. Ranson grinned. "Sure, Mat, Mom will take you. No problem."

Mat remembered his buddies, Nick, Nando, Al, Sam, and Sid as they had seen him off this morning at the airport. They had been almost as excited as Mat, and each of them had given Mat specific instructions as to what he was to see and do while he was in Memphis. His friends had been very supportive of his steamboat design efforts all along.

Al had made sure that his computer specifications for the model were correct as they appeared on the blueprints. Al's teachers called him a computer whiz.

Memphis International was a huge airport and Mat felt as if he had entered another world. People with carriers scurried through wide hallways in time to arrive at gates that led to their far-flung destinations. Mat imagined all the different places where people would be traveling today. Intent on the excitement at the airport, Mat almost missed the escalator that went down to the baggage claim area.

"Come on, Mat," Mrs. Ranson encouraged, motioning him over to the down escalator. "Keep up with me or I'm going to have to get you a leash!" Mrs. Ranson was fun to be with and very supportive of all her students. She had lived in Memphis until she had gone to college, and knew nearly all the places and events happening there. She had even been cast as an orphan once at a professional theater in Overton Park, during one summer when she was a teenager. And that's how she had known about the riverboat design contest this weekend.

She had known Mud Island before it was such a tourist showcase.

Getting into the taxi at the airport, Mat felt renewed excitement. Mrs. Ranson gave the driver instructions, and they were on their way. There were three main routes to Mud Island including a Swiss monorail, a covered overhead walkway, and a riverboat. There was no doubt in Mat's mind which mode of transportation he wanted to use. He couldn't wait to board another riverboat!

Arriving at the riverboat dock, Mrs. Ranson glanced at her watch and calculated that they were on a very tight schedule. "We need to get on the 11:30 riverboat if we're to make the designers' luncheon at noon," she pressed. She threw her carry-on bag over her shoulder. "Mat, you get the rest of our luggage while I go get our riverboat tickets." She handed Mat a ten dollar bill to pay for the taxi. "Don't forget to get a receipt," she called out as she turned toward the riverboat ticket booth. Mat exited the cab, paid the driver, got the receipt and lugged the bags toward the ticket booth.

Approaching the booth, he noticed that the riverboat had already docked and people were boarding. Settling down for the short ride to the island, Mat could hear the tour guide on her microphone beginning her discourse on Mud

Island: "Opened just ten years ago this month, Mud Island is a fifty-acre, sixty million dollar entertainment and educational complex devoted to the preservation of the river, its ecology, its history, and its role as the great artery of American settlement and commerce.

"The riverboat will dock at the River Center, which houses a restaurant, a theater, and shops...."

Finally Mat began to breathe easily and relax. He was almost there. He opened a cellophane-wrapped candy and began to bite into its contents. Then it hit him. He looked quickly at every piece of luggage. The tube containing his blueprints was missing. He hit his head with his hand and turned to Mrs. Ranson. "The blueprints are missing, Mrs. R.! I left them on the rear-window shelf in the taxi!" He jumped up and reexamined the luggage pieces. "What'll I do! I can't be in the contest without them! What a dunce! Al will kill me! I'll never get them back. Never!"

After she had confirmed the worst, Mrs. Ranson put her hands over his shoulders and said, "Calm down, Mat. We'll figure out something. Did you get that receipt from the cab driver?"

Mat fiddled through his pants pockets, retrieved the receipt and gave it to Mrs. Ranson. Tears welled up in his eyes. He had worked so hard for this chance. And one silly mistake, just an instant's lapse of concentration, might ruin it for him.

"Just as I expected," Mrs. Ranson said. "This receipt has the address and phone number of the cab company. It's a long shot," she admitted, "but when we get to the island, I'll drop you off at the luncheon and telephone the cab company. Surely, no one would want a set of blueprints. If they can get in touch with the cab driver, my mother or father may be able to get the prints before they meet us this evening. I feel sure the judges will understand and wait until then to review your blueprints. You do have the prototype, don't you?"

"It's right here," Mat assured her, holding tight to the box bearing his model. His despair subsided. He was trying to calm down. An enormous cloud cast a shadow over one entire side of the boat, and Mat felt sure it was an abject sign of things to come.

He felt helpless sitting there listening to the tour guide's lecture, and wanted to crawl into a big hole and disappear. What a jerk! His friends would never forget this one! After all that work . . . .

Some tough-looking men tied the riverboat to its pilings at the dock. Then the passengers trampled over the rough-hewn gangplank to the River Center. Once on the dock, Mat and Mrs. Ranson spotted a large sign with an arrow leading them toward the designers' luncheon area. As they neared the area, Mrs. Ranson spoke calmly to Mat, "As soon as we meet the program chairperson, I'll explain what has happened. I feel sure he'll understand. I'll ask to be excused from the luncheon. Then I'll be back after I can get some word on the lost blueprints. Don't worry, Mat. Everything will work out."

Welcoming Mat and Mrs. Ranson at the door of the restaurant was Mr. Josephson, the program chairperson. "Ah, you must be Mat Miller," he greeted them, holding out his hand to shake. "Fred Josephson here. And you must be Mrs. Ranson," he said as he turned to shake her hand. "Everyone else has arrived. Do come and join us."

"Mr. Josephson," Mrs. Ranson began, "Could we please have a word with you before we join the others? It's an emergency."

Mr. Josephson sensed the concern in her voice. "Certainly," he replied. "What can I do for you?"

"Well," Mrs. Ranson confided, "Mat left the blueprints for his model in the taxi not twenty minutes ago."

"What?" Mr. Josephson reacted. "He must be devastated to come so far and lose his plans less than a mile away!"

"We do have a receipt naming the cab number and time of the ride. I'm hoping we can get them back. So I would like to phone the cab company. As you can understand, Mat is very upset about the situation and would like to have the judging of his model be postponed until we can get a handle on the blueprints' whereabouts."

"I'm sorry to hear about your situation, Mat," Mr. Josephson remarked. "I'll do everything I can to help."

"Thank you, sir," Mat replied.

With that, Mrs. Ranson left Mat with Mr. Josephson and went into the center's main

office area to make her phone calls.

"Let's hope everything will work out, Mat," Mr. Josephson said, putting his arm around Mat's shoulder and leading him into the luncheon area. "I'll give you the royal treatment while we wait."

Mat was in awe of the restaurant's decor. An authentic reconstruction of the front third of an 1870s riverboat, it stood three stories high. He walked into the grand salon.

As soon as Mat met the other boat designers and saw the food he almost forgot his troubles.

"Pretty good, huh, Mat?" Mr. Josephson boasted.

"It's terrific," Mat answered. "Just being here is a once in a lifetime thrill. I love riverboats!" Mat began telling Mr. Josephson all about his dad, the Fish Shack, and all the riverboat models they had put together.

It was nearly an hour before Mrs. Ranson got back to the restaurant. "Mat," she started, pulling him aside, "I don't want you to get upset, but I still can't get in touch with the cab driver. I telephoned the cab company and the operator told me that there was absolutely nothing she could do for me. So I called Dad, gave him the name and number of the cab driver, and asked him to go to the cab company directly and speak to the owner before coming here."

Mat could feel butterflies welling up inside his stomach again. But there was nothing he could do but wait. So he decided to make the best of it. After all, he was aboard one of the first riverboat museums in the world.

Mat began introducing Mrs. Ranson to the other competitors. People smiled at Mat. Some offered their sympathy. By now, everyone had heard that his plans were lost. Being here among the finalists at the national contest was a moment Mat had dreamed of since he was seven years old. Suddenly, being here among the other finalists was the hardest thing he'd ever done.

The judges moved slowly past each model. They stopped here and there, murmuring among themselves.

Around 6:30, all the judging had been completed, except for Mat's blueprints. The judges were whispering among themselves. A judge walked to the microphone. Mr. Josephson looked regretfully at Mat. "Ladies and gentlemen," he began. Mat stood still, a look of absolute hopelessness on his face. People were becoming impatient. He could see it on their faces, behind their polite smiles. "They all believe I'm a fool," Mat thought to himself. "They probably wonder how somebody as stupid as me could even get into the contest." Deep in thought, Mat didn't realize that every other head in the room had turned toward the back entrance. Someone was shouting. Mrs. Ranson's father came running into the exhibit area. "I've got your prints, Mat," he called.

Mr. Josephson noticed the excitement and rushed to the judges. After a pause, the judge said, "I thought we had completed the judging, but it seems as if young Mr. Miller's plans have been rescued." The entire audience applauded.

Mat sprinted with the blueprints toward the judges. He tried to hide his excitement, but there was no use. He grinned from ear to ear as he handed them the prints. "We're awfully glad to see

these, Mat," they replied. "We really couldn't hold up the judging a minute longer." The judges huddled again to review their decisions.

Mrs. Ranson's father, Mr. Phelps, explained what had happened. "I never got to the cab company," he said. "I went home and noticed that there was a message on my answering machine. It was from your dad, Mat. It seems that a man from Audubon Park had accidentally picked up the blueprints in the cab. He took them home and called the number on the package label."

"He called my home?" Mat wondered.

"Yes," Mr. Phelps went on, "and your dad phoned me. I rushed over to Audubon Park, got the blueprints and barely made the 6:00 monorail ride to the center."

Just as the judges were about to reveal the winners, Mrs. Ranson's mom arrived. She couldn't believe what had happened. "It just goes to show you," Mrs. Phelps declared, "People in big cities have hearts after all!"

A hush came over the crowd as a judge stepped up to the microphone. "The winner of the Mud Island Tenth Anniversary Riverboat Design Contest is Joseph Graph, for his model, *Island Beauty*," he announced. "And the runner up goes to an outstanding youngster, Mat Miller, with his very first entry, *The Modern Memphis*. Would the gentlemen please come up and accept their trophies?"

Mrs. Ranson and her parents clapped joyfully as Mat approached the stage to receive his second-place trophy. His face lit up like a five-hundred-watt light bulb.

Later, when the crowd had dispersed, Mat and the Phelpses strolled along Mud Island's River Walk. At last, Mat's eyes viewed all its glory. "Well," Mrs. Ranson announced as they walked back over the riverboat's gangplank, "I'm prepared to veg out. I'm exhausted."

"What about dinner?" Mat hinted, his eyebrows pointing upward. "Man, I've never been this hungry before. You wouldn't want me to starve, would you?"

Vocabulary Expansion

Define and describe these words and phrases:

up in arms	indelibly printed	chairperson
first entrant	Graceland	grand salon
prophetic	tourist showcase	regretful look
neophyte	discourse	in a new light
pilot house	lapse of concentration	Elvis Presley
specifications	thrill of a lifetime	asphalt
carry-on bag	make the best of it	paddle wheel
confirm	veg out	Overton Park
abject sign	fireballs	tight schedule
mill about	chaperone	breathe easy
starve to death	euphoria	prototype
have a big heart	monorail	butterflies
Andrew Jackson	preserve	small world

Language Expansion Activities

1. Pick a city in the United States and write a composition about it. Use facts from various sources such as the Internet, encyclopedias, historical pamphlets, brochures, and travel guidebooks. Let your writing convince the others in your group that they should go to this city. Compare your composition with the compositions of others in your group. List the cities in the order in which you would like to visit them based on everyone's reports.

2. Write a folded brochure (use photographs or other visuals if you wish) about the city you've researched in activity number one. If you have access to a computer, let your teacher help you with the layout. If not, use the cut-and-paste technique. Pretend you will receive a large commission for everyone you can convince to visit your city.

Language Expansion Questions

1. Where was Mat going? Why?

2. Why did Mat need a chaperone? Have you ever had a chaperone? What was the occasion?

3. Did Mat win the contest? What lesson did he learn? Have you ever lost a contest but won something even greater? Explain.

4. Mat's momentary lapse of concentration got him into trouble in this story. Has daydreaming ever gotten you into trouble?

5. Pretend you are interviewing the winner of the contest and tell all about his entry, *Island Beauty*. Write a list of questions you will ask him.

6. Predict what would happen if this story continued. Write the new ending.

7. The judges were ready to make their announcement just before Mat's blueprints arrived. Discuss whether or not they should have held up the judging at all. How did the other contestants feel about it?

8. The story made mention of many facts about Memphis. Name as many as you can remember. Find out more about Memphis in your library or on the Internet. Would you like to go to Memphis? Why?

9. Identify the point at which Mat became the most frustrated. Have you ever been that frustrated? Why?

10. Create a new adventure for Mat. Be sure to include directions for him to follow in his own way. Will he forget something? Will he become frustrated? How can these things help a story become more interesting?

Unit 48

KNOWING RIGHT FROM WRONG

UNIT 48

Phonology/Orthography Concepts

- Phonograms are letter groups that usually represent the same sounds (phonemes).
- At the beginning of a word, the phonogram **kn** represents the phoneme /n/.
- At the beginning of a word, the phonogram **wr** represents the phoneme /r/.

Vocabulary

knack	knitting	wrangle	wring	*front*
knapsack	knob	wrangler	wrinkle	*view*
knee	knobby	wrap	wrist	
kneecap	knock	wrath	wristband	
kneeling	knockout	wreath	write	
knell	knot	wreck	writhe	
knew	knothole	wreckage	writing	
knickknack	knotting	wrench	written	
knife	know	wrestle	wrong	
knight	knowledge	wretch	wrought	
knighthood	known	wretched		
knit	knuckle	Wright		

KNOWING RIGHT FROM WRONG

Story Summary:

A couple of old acquaintances of Ted's provide Sam Webster with one of his greatest adventures–and a terrifying experience. In the process, Sam discovers that some people really don't know the difference between right and wrong.

Sam felt a chill crawl up his spine. He'd had a front row view of the events that had taken place on the dock outside Jen Wells' Pet Shop. Kneeling inside the door of the shop to keep himself hidden, he realized that his knuckles  had turned white from clenching his fists so tightly. As the sun dipped into the water on the horizon, he checked the time. The watch on his wrist said 6:30.

Jen Wells had left early this Saturday, leaving Sam to finish sweeping and locking up. Sam had been working at the Pet Shop on Saturdays for more than a year now, earning extra pocket money.

People had always felt safe around the dock. Everybody in town visited the shops there; it was a popular meeting spot for people of all ages. But at this very minute, Sam didn't see another soul. In the silent sunset, he heard the tinkling wind chimes from Ted's Shell Shop next door. The spring wreath on the Pet Shop's front door thunked like a knoll outside.

He'd hoped that his friend, Mat Miller, might still be working at his parents' Fish Shack. Then he remembered that Mat was in Memphis. Sam couldn't see down that far anyway, and he was afraid to get up and run to the phone. Sam had been kneeling so long that he'd lost all feeling in his knees and could hardly move. But he managed to crouch over and grab the knife Jen kept behind the counter for opening boxes. The knowledge that he had a knife to defend himself was not much comfort. A knot formed in Sam's stomach. He felt wretched. He knew what he'd heard was a shot.

Holding his head up just high enough to peek out the front window of the shop, Sam spotted the elderly man writhing on the ground. It was the  same man who had docked his yacht there at noon. Earlier, he'd seen the man outside the Shell Shop chatting with Ted.

Now the man lay sprawled on the dock. There was no one else in view. Only an hour earlier, Ted, the sailor whose Shell Shop was next to Jen's, had been sitting outside on a bench knotting lines for his houseboat. Now there was nobody. Nothing moved. Sam knocked on the wall of the shop, hoping that Ted would hear him, but there was no response. Ted must have gone home, too.

There was nobody else to help the man. Nobody. Sam Webster had never felt quite so alone.

He could sneak out the back door of the shop, hop on his bike, and hightail it home—but Sam knew right from wrong. Right now, Sam remembered something his grandfather had told him again and again: "Sometimes, wrong is easier than right. The trouble is, you have to live with yourself afterward."

Sam Webster knew the right thing to do. First, he called 911. Then he unlatched the front door. He wrapped himself in courage, tried to ignore his knocking knees, and strode out toward the man lying on the dock. The air was still. The only sound he heard was the water lapping up against the sides of boats. The sun had slipped into the western sky, and a thin blanket of darkness covered everything.

The man didn't appear to be moving. Sam felt his pulse and realized that he was still alive. "Help is on the way, sir," Sam assured him.

"Right," he heard the man say. "Right!" The man kept whispering it. Sam saw his wrist moving in circles. "Right!" he rasped again, insistently.

"Oh! You mean write! You mean you want to write something! I've got a pencil someplace, I think." Sam dug into his jeans pocket and found the stub of a yellow pencil he'd used in the shop that day. "Here, sir. Do you think you could write your name?"

On a wrinkled scrap of paper Sam dug out of his pocket, the man wrote, WRECK. Sirens broke the silence. Sam could hear police and ambulance sirens. They were responding to his 911 call. It seemed like it had been hours, but when he looked at his wristwatch, it was just 6:40. He tucked the scrap of paper into his pocket and rushed up to greet the police car. "I think he needs help quick," Sam said. "He can barely talk!"

After the ambulance left, Sam realized that wretched knot in his stomach had not gone away. Every time he got nervous, Sam could feel it in his stomach. He got on his bike and headed home.

Sometime shortly after the Websters had finished dinner and washed the dishes, the doorbell rang. "I'll get it," sighed Sam's mom. "Neither of you two will get up from that basketball game anyway. You didn't hear the doorbell, did you? You don't hear me, do you?" It was a Webster family game. When

Sam and his dad watched basketball, they blocked out everything else.

But they both perked up soon. Jen Wells had come to inquire about Ted. "Sam, I had invited Ted to dinner with the other shop owners from the dock. Remember? That's why I left early, so I could get home and get everything ready for our dinner and meeting. Everybody else arrived by 7:00, but Ted never showed up!" Jen was a wreck.

"Chick Miller went over to Ted's houseboat," Jen continued, "and he found Ted's front latch open. No sign of Ted. We called the police, but they can't file a missing persons report 'til someone's been missing more than twenty-four hours! I'm worried. I thought there was a chance Sam might know what happened to Ted."

Sam told Jen what had happened at the dock just before he had left. He told her about the sound of a shot. He told her about seeing the man lying alone on the dock. He told her about knocking on the wall of Ted's Shell Shop and getting no response. "I thought Ted had left early," Sam told her. "I knew you had a shop owners' meeting tonight. And I remembered you saying Ted was doing the cooking. So I didn't even go into his shop before I left the dock."

"Do you have any idea who the man was, Sam? Had you ever seen him before?" Jen was wringing her hands. "Did you actually think you heard a shot?"

"It sounded like a shot, but there wasn't any blood anywhere," Sam responded.  "Do you remember that man Ted was talking to this afternoon? You met him. The man who had just docked his yacht in the harbor?"

"Oh, Sam! Why didn't somebody call me? That man is Ted's old friend, Ben Wright! I've got to get to the hospital. Maybe he can help us find out what happened to Ted!" Jen Wells rushed out of the Webster house without another word.

Sam felt terrible. It hadn't occurred to him or to his parents to call Jen and let her know what had happened at the dock. "Dad," he suggested, "Maybe we could go out and see if we could find some sign of Ted."

At the hospital, Jen discovered that Ben Wright had been taken into critical care. He had apparently suffered a heart attack. "Has an elderly gentleman named Ted by chance been in here to see Mr. Wright?" Jen inquired of the critical care nurse. No one at the hospital had seen or heard from anybody named Ted.

Jen recalled the stories Ted had told her about his friendship with two other sailors. The three had met years ago as young sailors going out to sea. For years, they had worked side by side. In later years, Ben Wright and Patrick Knowles had become charter boat captains, very successful men. When Ted retired from the service, he had opened Ted's Shell Shop at the dock. The three men had remained best friends for more than fifty years. There was one thing that the three still had in common. They were all bachelors. None of them had ever married. Neither Ben Wright nor Patrick Knowles had any family.

Jen was standing in the lobby of the hospital emergency room, trying to decide what to do next, when she heard the announcement.  *"Will the person who inquired about Mr. Ben Wright please come to the nurses' station? Will the person who inquired about Mr. Ben Wright please come to the nurses' station?"*

"That was all he said," the nurse explained to Jen.

"Just before Mr. Wright died, he kept whispering the same words to me over and over again: "*wreck . . . wreck . . . wreck.*"

As Jen was getting into her van, the Websters' car slid into the space next to hers. Sam's beloved lab,  Eagle, jumped out of their car and into Jen's lap. "I forgot something, Jen!" Sam told her. "It's this paper. Mr. Wright wrote something on it just before the ambulance came. I thought it might help us find Ted!" Sam showed Jen the wrinkled scrap of paper that read simply, *WRECK.*

"We've got to get this to the police, Sam," insisted Jen. "This is the same word that Ben Wright kept repeating to the nurse just before he died. I don't know what it means, but maybe they can help us figure it out. We've just got to find Ted. We've just got to!" Since her own father had died, Ted had become much like a second father to Jen Wells. She loved him more than anybody realized.

"I'll tell you what, Jen," suggested Mr. Webster, Sam's father. "What if you take that note down to the police station and explain to them about Mr. Wright's last words."

"We'll head down toward the dock," Mrs. Webster added. "You can meet us down there. Sam just had an excellent idea. He said we need to get into Ted's Shell Shop and see if Ted could be inside!"

Old-fashioned gas lights lit the renovated dock area at night, casting eerie shadows over land and water. Since the shops all closed at 5:30 on Saturdays, the area had been empty for several hours now. Sam's dad pulled the car up into the nearest parking space and the Websters rushed toward Ted's Shell Shop.

Mrs. Webster was worried. The Websters had become close to Ted over the past several months. Sam had a Saturday job at Jen Wells' Pet Shop next door to Ted. She understood why Jen and the Millers and the other shop owners were so fond of Ted. Nobody could tell a story like Ted! "Poor Ted," she murmured sympathetically. "He has no family. He really doesn't have anybody except Jen and us! We have to find him!"

The front door of Ted's Shell Shop was locked. There were no lights on inside, and it was impossible to see in. "Let's try the back door," suggested Sam. "Back where I park my bike. Ted's back door is next to Jen's."

The door wasn't latched. Once inside the musty storeroom behind the Shell Shop, Sam found the candle Ted kept on the shelf near the back door. They lit it and entered the Shell Shop cautiously.

Sam spotted Ted first. Lying on the floor, bound and gagged, Ted's head was inside the kneewell of his rolltop desk.

"Look, Dad! On the shelf under the cash register! Ted keeps his whittling knife under there. Let's get him untied!" cried Sam.

"Hold on for just a minute," Mrs. Webster assured the old man. "Who in the world did this to you?"

Kneeling beside him, Mr. Webster sliced the ropes that had been used to tie Ted up. "These look like lines," he commented, as he examined the frayed edges.

"They are. Aye. They are," Ted noted, rubbing his wrists and knees, where he had been bound. "Those lines belong to Ben Wright, my old sailing mate. He left them with me. I was reworking them for him."

Sam glanced at his mother. They had to tell Ted about the fate of his old shipmate. Mrs. Webster hated telling Ted, but she knew they had to do it.

"Ted, why don't you let us help you onto your chair and you can tell us what happened here?" Together, they helped Ted up. Sam got him a cup of water from the storeroom.

"It was just as I was closing up," Ted recalled. "About 5:30, I heard a shot outside. Unmistakable sound. I'd turned off the lights. Was about to lock up when I heard my front door creak. I heard those little bells tinkling. The bells over the front door. I looked up front, but it was dusk and it was hard to see."

"Could you see who it was?" Sam asked. "I didn't see anybody."

"That's just the thing, Sam," Ted replied. "I didn't see anybody either. I came back up front, and there wasn't anybody there. Didn't hear another sound. So I put the latch on the front door and started to leave. I started for the back door. Something hit me over the head. I blacked out. That's the last thing I remember.

"Later, I woke up under the desk," Ted continued. "It seemed like a long time until you all came in."

"Whoever it was left from the back, Ted," Sam offered. "The front door was locked when we got here." Just then, they heard voices outside, and were glad to see Jen Wells and a detective at Ted's front door.

"Thank heaven! Ted!" shouted Jen Wells, flipping on the overhead lights in the Shell Shop. Jen hugged Ted. The detective opened the front window of the shop.

After Sam and Ted had related everything they knew, Detective Rozas went into the storeroom. A few minutes later, he came out with a small, worn black leather book. "I found this just outside the back door," said the detective. "Mean anything to you, Ted?" he asked.

Ted looked at it and shook his head. Opening the front cover, he whispered, "P. Knowles. This book belongs to my old mate. Patrick Knowles. Patrick and Ben Wright and I have been mates for more years than I can count. I hadn't heard from them for two years.

"Then today, Ben Wright came to see me. He said he and Patrick were being threatened by a man named Jake. Terrible trouble. This Jake was after them to do something illegal. Not Ben and Patrick. They're honest mates. Ben left here and went out looking for Patrick. Ben thought they could get the Coast Guard after this man Jake. If Ben even found Patrick, he never got back here to tell me." Ted was distraught.

"Ted," Jen interrupted. "There's something I have to tell you. It's about your friend, Ben Wright . . . ." After she told Ted, she hugged him. The shop became silent, except for the sound of the bells tinkling as the night air wafted in through the shop windows.

"Oh, no!" They heard a voice moaning, "Oh, no!" The voice had come from the storeroom. Everybody looked toward the back of the shop, frozen.

An elderly man appeared from the darkness. Rags bound his upper arm, his shirt covered in blood. "Ted!" he cried, "I hope you can forgive me, old mate! I hid in your closet while Jake was here. He shot me, but just grazed my arm. I must have passed out. The next thing I knew, I heard someone saying Ben was dead. Poor Ben!" The man was Patrick Knowles.

"Maybe you can help us find out where this Jake is now," declared Detective Rozas. "You may know something that could help us find him."

"Ben and I met Jake last May," Patrick told them. "Jake was greedy. Eager to get rich. He told us about a shipwreck he'd heard about, south of Miami. He wanted us to help him retrieve the bounty from the wreck. But when Ben and I  looked into it, we discovered that the ship was still the property of a Spanish company. We had no right to it. But Jake wouldn't let it go. People like Jake don't know right from wrong."

"So what happened then?" Sam inquired.

"Well, he kept after us 'til late last week. He threatened to force us to take him to the sunken wreck to retrieve the bounty. He sounded dangerous. We got on Ben's yacht and sailed up here. Our plan was for Ben to stay with Ted while I went undercover. I met with a Coast Guard officer who said that they'd been after Jake for five years. Said he's robbed other ships. They even suspect him of murder. I was supposed to meet Ben back at the dock at 5:30, but I was late." Patrick Knowles slumped into a chair, exhausted.

"When I got to the dock," he continued, "I found Ben lying there. That's when somebody took a shot at me. I escaped and hid in Ted's closet. But just as I closed the closet door, I saw Jake sneak into the front door and hit Ted over the head from behind. He must have thought Ted was me. That's when I passed out."

"Now it all fits together," commented Detective Rozas. "Ben Wright kept repeating *'wreck'*."

"Right," added Patrick. "We kept the records of Jake's threats aboard Ben's yacht. Ted would have figured it out all right . . . ." Patrick was interrupted by the shrill sound of a ship's siren. Everybody looked out front and viewed two Coast Guardsmen dragging a handcuffed man toward the Coast Guard cutter.

"Looks like we'll all have a safe night," Patrick commented, nodding toward the cutter. "That cutter's on its way to the brig!"

Vocabulary Expansion

Describe and define these words and phrases:

you have to live with yourself
a front row view	she was a wreck	yacht
clenching his fists	chill crawled up his spine	critical care
pocket money	a blanket of darkness	bachelors
broke the silence	know right from wrong	second father
hightail it home	pulled the car up	horizon
shop owners	double bolt lock	storeroom
cutter	rolltop desk	kneewell
closing up	retrieve the bounty	brig
	wringing her hands	charter boat

Language Expansion Activities

1. Make a list of all the events that took place beginning at 5:30 on Saturday afternoon. Refer to the text to be certain that your list is in the correct sequential order. Then, explain how the story might have changed if events had happened in a different order.

2. Find a reference book and gather all of the information you can about the role of the Coast Guard. What are the responsibilities of the Coast Guard? What kind of work do they do? Where is their work done? Explain the differences between the Coast Guard and other military branches.

Language Expansion Questions

1. How much time went by between the beginning of the story and the time that the police and ambulance arrived?

2. Why had all the shop owners left early that Saturday?

3. The only clue to Ted's whereabouts was a single word. What was it? Where did Sam and Jen get the clue?

4. Why was Sam hiding in the Pet Shop when the story began? What frightened him? Why did he decide to go outside?

5. Where had Sam first seen the man he found on the dock?

6. What did the man on the dock try to tell Sam? What happened to the man?

7. Sam thought about a "knot in his stomach." He said that every time he got nervous, the knot came back. Have you ever experienced that feeling? What are some of the things that have caused you to have the feeling?

8. The story said that Ted had been like a "second father" to Jen Wells. Explain what that means. How did Jen feel about Ted?

9. When the Websters arrived at the Shell Shop, the front door was locked, but the back door was unlatched. Explain the events that had resulted in this strange situation.

10. How had Jake been threatening Ben and Patrick? At the end of the story, Patrick said, *"Looks like we'll all have a safe night. That cutter's on its way to the brig!"* Explain what Patrick meant by this statement.